Identifying an Area of Expertise for Your Blog

Perhaps the most important aspect of starting a blog and becoming a professional blogger is the process involved in identifying the focus of your blog. The single biggest mistake beginning bloggers make is failing to identify a specific focus, instead choosing to write about whatever happens to come into their mind at any given moment. This is good as a strategy for writing practice, but it is very unlikely to win you any regular readers or to help you build a core audience for your burgeoning writing career.

If you want to be a professional blogger like me, Dana Sibilsky, focus on one subject and adhere to it closely. Sure, you can occasionally delve into a topic that is only somewhat relevant to your core focus every once in a while, but you have to ensure that your audience knows exactly what they are getting each time they type in your web address or, even better, click on the bookmarked tab that links to your site. So, how do you go about choosing a subject that will attract and engage readers on a regular basis?

It is important to recognize that there is a danger in pandering to the audience. Too many bloggers – professional or otherwise – get caught up in their web analytics and then focus only on writing about the subjects that perform best. This is why you see so many "Top 10" sites – it's well known that an article organized in list form is better "click bait" than any other format. While this strategy works in some regards, you are much better off building a core group of devoted readers who keep coming back for your insight on a specific subject.

To build this core group of devoted readers, you have to be working with the right subject. Identifying the most ideal subject matter is not necessarily as simple as you may think, so ask yourself the following questions before making a choice:

- How well do you know your subject?
- Do you care deeply about your subject?
- Are you willing to take a side on divisive issues relating to your subject?
- How much time do you already spend reading and discussing the subject?
- Why is this subject important to you?
- What topics will you discuss in your first five posts?

Before you start answering these questions, allow me to explain why it is important to ask each question in the first place and how each one relates to the success or failure of your professional blogging career.

How Well Do You Know Your Subject?

It should be abundantly clear that you should be exceptionally knowledgeable when it comes to a subject you plan to write about on a regular basis, but this is actually something of a point of contention among professional bloggers. I have spoken with writers who insist that a professional blogger should essentially be an "online scholar," whose education or relevant experience could easily qualify them to teach the subject at the undergraduate level, at minimum. Other writers I have discussed this with have said that bloggers are essentially entertainers and their knowledge of the subject matter is secondary to their ability to entertain their readers.

I disagree with both of these extreme opinions.

When it comes to your knowledge of the subject, I feel that you should just know it well enough to engage an expert in a five-minute conversation. If your subject is philosophy and you can confidently discuss the work of Rene Descartes for five minutes with an adjunct professor, that is more than enough knowledge of the subject matter to feel confident in blogging about it. The same goes for any other subject, whether it is fine art, politics, sports or arts and crafts. If you can briefly but confidently discuss the respective subject with an artist, a politician, an athlete or a crafting expert, then you can blog about it too.

There will certainly be instances in which a bit of research is required, but this is true of all writing in general. The key is that you have a basis of knowledge upon which you can draw and that you are able to make inferences and connections between what you already know and what you discover through research. Of course, you do have to be engaging and entertaining, but we will discuss that more in-depth in a later chapter.

Do You Care Deeply About Your Subject?

This is an incredibly important question and one that is very deserving of thorough consideration. If you are going to start a blog with the intention of making a career out of it, you must be passionate about the subject you choose. Successful blogs offer a minimum of three to four posts per weeks, with the most popular blogs offering a new post daily. This can become a bit of a grind even when you care deeply for the subject matter, so be careful to avoid something that may only be a passing interest.

The other consideration to take into account is the fact that it is difficult for a writer to hide the fact that they are dispassionate about a subject. When your subject matter is truly important to you, it will be clearly evident to readers. The opposite is also true, so if you pick a subject you know to be popular in an effort to attract more readers, the fact that you are not wholly invested in the subject will actually turn them away. Do yourself and your readers a favor by choosing something that is deeply important to you.

Are You Willing to Take a Side on Divisive Issues Relating to Your Subject?

Even the most mundane subject matter is sure to have divisive issues crop up from time to time, and professional bloggers cannot always position themselves on both sides of the issue. At some point you will have to take a position that is unpopular with a large portion of your readers, and you cannot fear that doing so will alienate them or drive them away. Taking a position and presenting well-reasoned arguments will actually be quite endearing to your readers, especially to those who disagree.

No subject is free of divisive issues, so you have to be willing to present a clear and concise viewpoint in support of your position. You will also have to engage your readers who disagree – not with the goal of convincing them otherwise, just to demonstrate that you arrived at your position in a logical manner after considering a variety of perspectives. You have to be willing to take one side or another, because you will lose respect if you are always attempting to straddle a line.

How Much Time Do You Already Spend Reading and Discussing the Subject?

Blogging is a time-consuming affair, so you have to ask yourself how much more time you are willing to commit to a particular subject. If you use your free time to read contemporary philosophy or to argue about baseball on a regular basis, then the amount of additional time you spend researching for your philosophy or sports blog will not be so significant. If you haven't read up on philosophy since college or are only a casual sports fan, you may find that the time commitment required to professionally blog will swell quite a bit.

Why Is This Subject Important to You?

Answer this question in one sentence. Right now, answer it. Say it aloud or write it on a scrap piece of paper, but do it right now before reading another word.

Is it difficult to answer the question in one concise sentence? If it is, you may want to consider something else. If you were able to answer the question quickly and without much thought, you may very well be on the right track.

What Topics Will You Discuss in Your First Five Posts?

You can take a bit longer to consider this, but write down the topics you will discuss in your first five posts. You don't have to sketch out an outline or summarize anything, just write down five headlines. For example, a philosophy blog might have a title like, "The Grateful Dead and the Influence of Zen Buddhism." The sports blog might have a headline that reads, "How Advanced Analytics Have Changed the Way NBA Teams Use the Three-Point Line." Whatever subject you are considering, write down five headlines for your first five posts in the next 15 minutes or so.

Done?

Did the topics come into your mind without much thought, or did you find yourself struggling to come up with more than just one? As a blogger, you will have to come up with new topics on a daily basis, and there is nothing worse than trying to tap a well that has long since run dry. If you choose the right subject, your head will be just swimming with ideas at all times.

One thing that many beginning bloggers worry about is the presence of other blogs that cover the same subject. Don't concern yourself with how many other bloggers are covering a specific subject or how established they are. All you have to do to be a successful blogger is to offer your unique insights in your own unique way. If you commit to being yourself and being true to your readers you will succeed no matter how many other bloggers are out there covering the same subject.

Developing a Unique Voice

Voice is an incredibly important component of writing and it is also happens to be one of those things that is somewhat elusive. You have probably heard any number of famous authors talking somewhat abstractly about how it took them a good deal of time before they were able to "discover their voice," but perhaps you never really gave the concept of voice much thought. A professional writer – no matter what their chosen medium may be – should give this concept a great deal of consideration while actively working to cultivate it through their writing.

There are a variety of strategies that can be used in your daily writing practice that can be helpful in developing your unique voice, but it is equally important to revisit and re-read what you have written previously in order to gain a better understanding of voice and how it applies to your writing. The ultimate goal of developing voice is to reach a point in which the reader no longer requires a byline to recognize a piece that you have written, meaning that your voice is entirely your own and is therefore inimitable.

In order to properly develop your voice in writing you must first have a deep understanding of the concept. In this section I will discuss the ways in which voice can be defined while also offering some advice with regard to its continued development. I feel that it is also important to note how voice will benefit you as you seek to become a professional blogger and to also identify how to properly use voice to your advantage throughout your writing career.

What Exactly Is Voice?

Voice is the unique and distinctive manner in which a writer tells a story. This is not to be confused with style, as voice includes a variety of factors that go well beyond the way you structure sentences or organize information. Voice also includes the way you perceive the world around you and how you choose to relay what you perceive. In a lot of ways, a writer with a fully developed voice is able to access their subconscious and allow it to come through in their writing. Of course, developing your voice does not have to be this complicated, but it is nonetheless one of the most important things you can do as a writer.

Be Honest and Engaging

The best way to cultivate voice is to simply focus on writing in a straightforward and honest manner. Readers want to know and understand what it is you believe and why you happen to believe it, and being able to explain yourself in a way that is both honest and forthright is an important tool for you to have as a writer. While you may think of honesty and forthrightness in terms of what you write, it also applies to how you write it.

Honest writing is done without any pretense and comes across to the reader as natural and effortless. Any writer who has ever labored over a particular word choice or revised a single phrase over and over again knows that writing can often be anything but natural and effortless, but the fact remains that it must seem that way to the reader. When you write and revise, take great care to make choices that reflect your voice and simultaneously engage the reader.

Write to Inform, Not to Impress

As a professional blogger it is your job to both inform your readers and to ensure that they are engaged and entertained by the way you choose to present the information. Many writers mistake the goal of entertaining and engaging for the goal of impressing their audience. This can be a significant miscalculation that alienates readers and prevents you from ever developing a core group of readers, so make sure that you understand the difference.

Consider the following: Imagine you are at a party and decide to conduct an informal survey on the literary preferences of the attendees. Given the choice between reading say, William Faulkner's The Sound and the Fury or John Green's The Fault in Our Stars, most would undoubtedly choose Green's work of young-adult fiction to Faulkner's innovative masterpiece. This is because that while most would acknowledge that Faulkner's work is superior, it is also, at times, completely incomprehensible.

Rather than writing to impress a very narrow audience, instead endeavor to write clearly and concisely while focusing on the message rather than the way the message is delivered. This does not mean that you have to oversimplify your writing; it just means that you have to ensure that what you are trying to say is not obscured by how you are trying to say it.

Recognize Your Influences Without Ripping Them Off

Whether we realize it or not, we are all influenced by the voice and style of other authors and some of that influence will creep its way into our voice. I am guilty of this and most other authors are as well, and that is perfectly acceptable. When you first learn to speak you adopt patterns of speech based on those around you, which is why there are pronounced regional dialects and accents. This happens with writing as well, and it is often a subconscious occurrence.

The authors that you read most frequently will affect how you write and will influence what is still your own unique voice. While having varying influences is entirely all right, you must also be careful not to engage in imitation. A look at the world of sports blogging will reveal a whole host of Bill Simmons imitators, and a quick look at the world of political blogging will demonstrate countless misappropriations of even the most obscure of Hunter S. Thompson's work.

The next time you sit down to right a column on how the President's dogs are "decadent and depraved," or feel like weaving in countless pop-culture references that are only tenuously linked to the topic, take a moment to ponder a different approach. The reason Thompson and Simmons -- however disparate their voices may be -- are frequently imitated is because their voices are unique and honest. Try to be the one whose voice is imitated rather than the one who is imitating.

Identify a Goal and Write Fearlessly

When you finally sit down to write, make sure you do so with a specific goal in mind. Whether you intend on writing a post on how to crochet or a post on diplomatic relations between foreign countries, make sure you understand what you want to accomplish and what message you intend to get across. Once you have identified this, write fearlessly and without any regard for what the reader or anyone else might think. Just write what comes naturally until you have accomplished your goal.

This is how you write with fearlessness. Writers sometimes get caught up in what their audience might think or say in response to a statement and this is certainly natural (especially when your readers begin quoting lines out of context in the comments section to criticize you). You have to consciously avoid this consideration while writing your first draft. If you read your post again and you feel that something is too controversial or is at risk of being misinterpreted you can always make an edit to cut or clarify the statement.

Your Process Is Your Own

When I first started writing professionally, I had an editor who laid out a specific process she wanted me to follow while crafting a piece. I don't remember exactly what it was because, frankly, it didn't help at all. In fact, it made things harder on me. Whatever process you choose, use it and use it confidently. I know writers who obsessively edit and I know others who feel that their first draft is always their best draft (the latter authors still edit their work, but just to clean up grammar and clarify anything that is unclear).

I feel that I work best when I write freely from start to finish and then walk away and do something else before returning to what I have written. This gives me a fresh set of eyes and allows me to read and revise more effectively, but that does not mean this will work for you. Choose a process that makes you feel comfortable and stick with it, even if an editor asks you to do otherwise. As long as the final product meets their editorial standards, how are they going to know what process you used?

Allow Your Voice to Evolve Over Time

Your voice is uniquely your own, and one of the things that makes us human is our ability to change. This applies to our writing voice, as you should not fear the fact that your voice will evolve over time. This is a good thing, so don't get overly concerned if you notice that your writing is evolving. Go back and re-read your work from years gone by, but do not try to return to your voice of the past. Simply focus on writing honestly and fearlessly. Your readers will appreciate it.

Writing Skill Refinement

If you are interested in taking on a career as a professional blogger you probably understand that writing is the primary skill involved. Yes, you need to have an understanding of how to manage a website and how to use a writing platform (don't worry, we'll delve into that in a later chapter), but writing is the undeniably key skill you must possess and you must be willing to work on consistently. Writing refinement takes a great deal of practice and there will never be a time in your writing career when this practice becomes unnecessary.

Even the greatest writers spend a good deal of time practicing, and some of the best writers will tell you that they look at everything they do as somehow relevant to the practice of writing. A conversation with a passerby can be a study in dialogue, while watching a film can be help you understand the importance of even the subtlest imagery. Writing practice is all around us; it's just a matter of recognizing it for what it is.

Recognizing opportunities for writing practice, of course, is not always easily accomplished. When you watch a film you may not immediately understand that the solitary fly perched atop a bowl of fruit is intended as a symbol of death or decay. In fact, you may not even notice it is there, and if you do you may just think that someone in the scene left a window open. When you begin perceiving things through the writer's lens, however, you will start to notice all those seemingly minor details so that you are able to make any connections later on.

So beyond paying close attention to the world around you and thinking of the ways you can make use of a snippet of dialogue, what other ways are there to practice and refine your writing? There are countless methods, and not all will necessarily be appealing to you in particular. Just like the writing process you employ, your practice should also be uniquely your own. Consider the following as both general advice and as individual writing practice strategies and simply adopt what works best for you:

- Read often, and read attentively
- Devote small blocks of time to practice each day
- Take revising seriously, but don't agonize over it
- Welcome any and all feedback
- Own your mistakes and learn from them
- Appreciate the writing process

I have found that abiding by the preceding guidelines for writing practice has been extraordinarily helpful for my professional writing career, and I believe that understanding how to use these guidelines in practice can help anyone refine their writing skills and improve their ability to write consistently well.

Whatever You Read, Read It Closely

When I read anything, whether it is a novel, a newspaper, an instructional guide or even the description of a sitcom episode, I try to be mindful of how the piece is written and determine what the writer's goals were while they were writing the particular piece. This is something that most people have to consciously set out to do, as it can be easy to just pay enough attention so that you just get the "gist" of it. Writers who are attentive while reading the work of others begin to recognize the true depth of a work and can understand how to effectively utilize the many subtle tools available to writers.

When I read something -- especially creative writing, long form journalism and op-ed pieces -- I look for a few things in particular, including:

- Structural elements
- Patterns or callbacks
- General writing techniques

The structure of a long form piece of journalism is particularly interesting as the author has a lot of options in terms of introducing the subject, providing context, including alternate perspectives and building suspense. The way in which these pieces are structured can be identified through a process similar to reverse engineering, which may help you see how the author initially outlined their article.

I also look for patterns and rhetorical tools in the writing, which can also be a lot of fun. Sometimes you will see that a particular columnist's heavy reliance on a specific pattern or rhetorical device makes their writing seem stale. Without looking for the pattern, you may not have been able to pinpoint the problem. When you recognize this in the work of others, you will start to see it in your own work as well.

No matter what you read, read it attentively. Pay close attention to every bit of punctuation and try to hear the music of the words when they are read aloud so that when you read your own work you are able to do so critically.

Writing Practice Is Important

Here is the most common advice writers get from other writers: Write every single day, no matter what.

Writers do not have to adopt some sort of monastic devotion to the art of writing, though some do and it works very well for them. There are stories of great writers doing very odd things and I don't think they are necessarily suitable for everyone else -- or anyone else, for that matter. An example: Friedrich Schiller, a German poet and philosopher, kept a drawer in his desk filled with rotting apples because the pungent and overwhelming odor helped him focus on his work.

Here is my advice: Just think about writing every single day.

I keep a journal and I write in it just about every day. It is a small, plain notebook that fits neatly in any bag I carry, allowing me to write whenever the spirit moves me. I jot down ideas for blog posts and I write for pages on end about all of the inanities of my life. Sometimes, however, I don't write in it at all, and that is all right. I simply try to think about writing every day and I end up writing on most days.

The most important thing you can do, however, is to have a creative outlet that allows you to write without it being work. The most surefire way to burn yourself out is to throw all of your energy into your professional work. Ernest Hemingway had a practice that I employ as well: When you complete your writing for the day, always leave a bit left over for the next day so you know where you are heading and where you can start. Essentially, don't tap the well until it is dry; leave some water at the bottom so that the well is refilled by the next morning.

Read and Revise, But Don't Agonize

Everything that you publish should be revised to a degree. As I mentioned in an earlier chapter, I do know of writers who believe in the adage that, "the first draft is the best draft," but even those writers do not submit their work without first lightly editing what they have written. I don't necessarily recommend this style, but if you can make it work then more power to you.

I will revise an article or post several times over before I submit it to an editor or before I post it to my personal blog. I first look for grammatical errors and make any appropriate changes before re-reading again to look at phrasing and clarity. This works for me, but you should adopt a revising strategy that makes you feel the most comfortable with the work you produce. I will say this, however: There is a risk in revising too much, so be careful and avoid agonizing over your work. No matter how much you revise something it will never be perfect in the eyes of every reader.

Ask For Feedback and Welcome Any Advice (Even When It's Unsolicited)

When you are ready and you feel confident in your work, ask for feedback as often as possible. Ask your friends and family, other writers and anyone else that is willing and listen carefully to what they say. Ask that they are unflinchingly honest, and accept feedback for what it is: an opportunity to improve your work. Once you are established as a professional blogger, you will get plenty of feedback from readers in the comments section. Engage them, be friendly and always thank them for sharing their opinion, even when they tell you that you are terrible.

When You Make a Mistake, Own It

At some point, you will make a mistake. Whatever mistake you make, own up to it and learn from it. When you write frequently enough there will be a time when a glaring error slips by you and is published for the world to see. Take it in stride, be honest and endeavor not to let it happen again.

Appreciate the Process

If you are going to truly enjoy being a professional writer, you have to appreciate the beauty of the process. Sometimes a piece that you think is the best thing you have ever done will only be read by a handful of people, while a piece you didn't think all that highly of will go viral and be read in countries where it has to be translated into another language. The result is not what matters; it is the process of writing and refining your skills that makes writing enjoyable. Focus on the process and enjoy each and every moment as it happens.

Choosing the Best Web Hosting and Writing Platform

We have already covered the writing process in great detail, but professional blogging requires a fairly unique skill set in a lot of different regards. Not only do you have to have solid writing skills and an inherent ability to entertain, but you also have to be tech savvy in order to become a professional blogger with a serious readership. Of course, there are ways around this if you are not as technologically literate as you would like to be, but it is still exceptionally important to at least have an understanding of your options with regard to web hosting and the writing platform you choose.

In order to become a professional blogger you have to have a web presence that hosts all of your work and simultaneously functions as a promotional tool for your career as a writer. If you want to be taken seriously as a blogger you will have to utilize a web host and a writing platform that reflects a high level of professionalism through the appearance of the site and the ease with which it is used. If you do not properly invest in the appearance and functionality of your site you will find that readers will not stay on your site no matter how great your content may be.

If you don't have a lot of experience with the technological side of things, this may seem like a daunting task. It isn't. You have to adopt a patient approach and be willing to ask for help when you need it. I was not the most technologically savvy individual before

I began blogging professionally, but I found most of the answers to the questions I had with just a bit of research. When I couldn't find the answer I was looking for, I turned to tech support for assistance. Now I feel comfortable with all of the varied aspects of web hosting and have a deep understanding of many of the various writing platforms that are available. With a bit of time and effort, you will too.

Account for Your Personal Experience

When it comes time to choose a web host and a writing platform you should consider a number of factors before arriving at a decision. While the total cost is likely to be at the forefront of your mind, you should understand that cutting corners now may cost you dearly in the future. If your website crashes due to its inability to handle increased traffic or your site is hacked due to inadequate protection, there will be untold costs that result. While you may not lose the work you have posted, you will likely lose a significant portion of all those hard-earned readers. Look at the cost of the web hosting as an investment in your blogging future and understand that a bit of extra investment will pay off in the long run.

While cost should not be a significant factor in determining the most ideal web host or writing platform, your personal experience absolutely should. The functionalities you choose to invest in should specifically relate to your ability to utilize them efficiently. If you have web design experience, then it makes perfect sense to invest in the ability to customize your site according to your preferences. If you are new to designing a website, then you will want to invest in a host that will streamline the process of setting up your site for you. Most of the available site templates provide users with the ability to customize their site to some degree, so don't worry about using a popular site template; you will still be able to make it your own.

Research Available Web Hosts

You have to be cautious when conducting research on web hosts, as one of the ways that blogs make money is through the use of affiliate marketing. That is, the blogger promotes a specific product and directs readers to buy the product in exchange for a cut of the profit. Most sites have a disclaimer, but some are less scrupulous; it is up to you to exercise proper caution when conducting research.

The best way to do this is by researching all of the various specifications of the site hosts for the purpose of comparison. Research and consider each of the following while making a decision:

- Storage space
- Bandwidth
- Domains and subdomains
- Features and support
- Mobile capability
- Installation

Your individual needs as a blogger will determine how you prioritize the features each web host offers, but the preceding factors should be among the most important in determining which host is right for you.

Consult Other Professional Bloggers

Researching web hosts and platforms without assistance is a dicey proposition, so don't hesitate to consult other professionals who have experience. Reach out to a blogger whose site is well-run and easy to use and ask about their web host and their writing platform and why they made those specific choices. Most professionals in the blogging community are more than willing to compare notes and will be quite helpful in steering you in the right direction. Just be forthright when you ask and disclose exactly why you are inquiring about web hosting and writing platforms.

Think Long-Term

It is perfectly all right to focus on modest goals when you are first starting out, but you do have to realize the importance of thinking long-term as well. If you want your blogging career to grow you have to give it room to do so. This does not mean that you have to invest in ridiculous storage space right from the beginning, but you should choose a host that will allow you to easily expand when the time comes to do so. If you create a site that is built for a small audience then that is what you will get. If you create a site built for a large audience with the right features to keep readers on the site for extended periods of time, eventually you will have a devoted group of readers who will do your promotional work for you.

Choose the Most Ideal Writing Platform

There are a lot of writing platforms out there for you to choose from, including easily recognizable platforms like

WordPress, Blogger, Squarespace and Tumblr, along with smaller platforms that boast a more minimalist approach. If you are unfamiliar with the major platforms you should probably take some time to get used to them as you will likely encounter them over and over again throughout your writing career. An overwhelming majority of sites use WordPress (nearly every site I do freelance work for has used some iteration of WordPress), so if you have never used it before, I would recommend familiarizing yourself with it at some point.

While it is important to be familiar with the major platforms, the writing platform you choose is entirely up to you. As long as you are able to use the other platforms, it does not matter much what platform you use for your own professional blog. What does matter is that the platform suits you and allows you to accomplish precisely what you want to accomplish. If, for example, you like to include varying types of media in your post to supplement your writing, you will want to make sure that your platform can handle this. If you prefer a minimalist writing style and want your site to reflect that, there are plenty of platforms that are able to do so.

Strive to Create a Community

One of the great keys to succeeding as a professional blogger is to build a community that ensures readers stay on your site long after they have finished reading your post. Your post should be something that sparks a conversation and stimulates discussion among your readers, and that discussion should take place right on your site. When you choose a host and a writing platform, carefully consider the type of comment section that is compatible with the host and platform.

The commenting platform is more important than you may realize, as readers are quite picky when it comes to the type of comment section they use. They will not want to register a new username or wait for administrator approval, so opt for an established commenting platform that will allow users to login with an existing username so they can immediately comment on your site. A robust comment section is the easiest way to legitimatize a website, and it is important that you engage your readers through this platform as well if you wish to build a loyal readership.

Once you have your hosting and writing platform in place, you can begin the process of writing and staging your articles. There are "best practices" for staging, but I feel that it is more important to present your work in the way that feels best for you and best reflects your style and sensibilities. Readers tend to prefer familiarity, but when your work is consistently outstanding and unique, readers will flock to your site on a regular basis.

Building an Audience

One of the most difficult aspects relating to the initial stages of professional blogging is the task of building and maintaining a core readership to follow your regular blog posts along with any guest posts and any freelance assignments you happen to take on. Your core readers will sustain your blog and will help you secure additional writing opportunities, especially when the sites you write for see that your work will consistently bring in additional traffic. Building an audience is difficult, however, and it may take a great deal of patience on your end before you have a base of readers who keep coming back for more each and every day.

When I first started out as a blogger I found it very difficult to go around promoting my work in an effort to get more eyes on my website. Over time I realized that you have to engage in a bit of shameless self-promotion from time to time, but it is possible to promote your work in a way that does not feel like begging. There are several strategies you can use to promote your work, and I will discuss these strategies in greater detail in later chapters. First, it is important to understand why you should build an audience and how you can begin to do so through a simple focus on the quality of the work you produce.

A Loyal Readership Is Key to Sustained Success

You will be amazed to discover how quickly the Internet can forget about you. I had a popular site link to an article on my blog in the first month I started out and had over 30,000 pageviews in a single day. I tried to capitalize on this traffic by adhering to the guidelines I had created for myself by adding a new post each day. The following day my site was down to 3,000 pageviews, and the day after I was back down to 500. It was demoralizing at first, but then I realized that I picked up a lot of returning visitors to the site from those 30,000 views. Each time a popular site linked to something I had written or anytime I wrote a guest post I noticed a slight uptick in my core audience.

As my core group of readers began to swell, I noticed that I was getting a lot of site referrals from social media and from shared links. Eventually I had a large readership that was interested in reading anything that I had written regardless of whether it was something I posted to my site or if it was something I contributed to a different site. My patience in building a core group of readers opened up a lot of doors for me professionally, and my readers are often a wonderful source of topic suggestions (just make sure you give them credit if they come up with a great idea for you to write about!).

So building an audience and being patient in doing so are clearly important. But how do you go about doing it, and what strategies work best?

Strategies for Building an Audience

I know a lot of writers who had no trouble at all in building an audience, but there are countless others who struggled mightily while employing every strategy imaginable. The time it takes to build an audience will depend a bit on your social circle. If you are something of an extrovert and have a lot of social connections it should not be too hard to build an initial audience who will refer others to the work you are doing. If you are an introvert and keep to a small social group, you may find that it takes a bit more time to build a core audience. Either way, a patient approach that utilizes the following strategies will ultimately yield a sizable readership:

- Focus on the quality of the work you produce
- Politely engage your audience on a regular basis
- Build a "brand"
- Utilize social media to promote your work
- Write guest posts for other blogs
- Accept freelance assignments whenever possible

Out of all of the aforementioned strategies, it is most important to consistently produce quality work. Whether you convince one person to read your work or 1 million, it will not matter very much if the work they read is not consistently outstanding. No amount of promotion, advertising or even begging will keep readers coming back if they cannot appreciate and enjoy the work you are producing. Keep your primary focus on the writing and take a long-term view when it comes to your readership.

The Importance of Patience

It is undeniably discouraging to write post after post without seeing a significant uptick in traffic, but you should not give up so easily if this is the case. It can sometimes take some time for a blog to get noticed by the right people, and while you should be doing all that you can to get readers to your site, it is sometimes simply the case that you have to exercise patience in building a readership. If your blog is struggling along with just a hundred views per day for weeks on end, think of it this way: How would you feel if you brought your work to a public reading and the room was packed with 100 people each and every night just to hear you read your work? You should be thrilled to have such an audience and you wouldn't even have time to individually thank them for being there!

Be grateful that you have a forum in which people can access your best work. There was a time when I was complaining about how much work I had put into a low-paying assignment when a friend reminded me of something Kurt Vonnegut had said to his son Mark after he made a similar complaint: "What would it have cost you to take out a two-page ad announcing you can write?" Keep things in perspective and be patient when it comes to building your audience. If your work is good and you care about your subject, you will build an audience that will read your work for many years to come.

Quality Work Should Always Be the Primary Consideration

There are many byproducts of impatience, and many of these byproducts sacrifice the quality of your writing and your standards in exchange for pageviews. While 1,000 pageviews in a single day is, mathematically speaking, greater than 100 pageviews in a day, if the work is not up to par those readers will not return. Many bloggers, especially those who are just getting started, quickly learn the strategies to impatiently boost the number of visitors reading their work. These are the strategies you should avoid at all costs:

- Writing intentionally inflammatory commentary
- Using misleading headlines
- Adopting extreme viewpoints without much basis for doing so (sometimes referred to as a "hot take")
- Arguing an unpopular position just for the sake of argument

These strategies will get people to read your work once, but you will quickly lose respect and very few people will take your work seriously in the future. If you use these strategies and manage to build a solid readership, you can be sure that someone will bring up something that you wrote in the past to make you look bad. Write with integrity and write what you believe in. Even if it takes more time to build a large readership it will have been worth the effort to ensure that you begin your career with your reputation intact and your integrity firmly in place.

You never want to write with an ulterior motive, so ensure that the goal of your writing is not based on how to attract more readers or how to grab a lot of attention in a short period of time. Produce work that is consistently outstanding and your readership will ultimately grow in a significant way.

Engage Your Audience in the Comments Section

Some writers feel as though they are above the comments section and do not ever bother to venture there, and there is certainly a case to be made for avoiding the comments section. I feel, however, that engaging your readers in polite conversation is an excellent way to establish a loyal readership base. The key here is to make sure that you are thoughtful in your responses and that you maintain a sense of professionalism at all times.

It is exceptionally valuable for readers to know that not only does your site offer access to your work but that it also offers access to you, the author. This is an opportunity to engage your readers in intelligent discourse and to clarify anything that your post may have left unclear. Your readers will appreciate being able to speak with you directly, and they will certainly appreciate it if you are kind and respectful no matter the circumstance.

If a reader asks a silly question, simply answer it as best you can without insulting them by criticizing the question. If someone is critical of something you wrote, thank them for the feedback as politely as possible. They did, after all, take the time to respond to your post, so take the time to respond to them and win them over with your kindness and your open mind to critical feedback.

The Importance of Positive Brand Development and Promotion

As a professional blogger your duties are sometimes going to be a bit all-encompassing. Not only are you a writer, you are also a PR specialist, a web designer, a community moderator and so much more. Though your responsibilities are many, it's not really all that daunting and taking on tasks that you may not necessarily be used to can actually be a lot of fun. One of these tasks is that of self-promotion, and it is fortunately the case that promoting yourself and creating a brand is so much more nuanced than just going around telling everyone how great you are.

When you write and post something new to your blog, you have to take steps to let people know that it's there and that it is worth reading. You cannot simply expect readers to magically appear on your website to read your latest work; it just doesn't work that way. You have to promote your work across a variety of social media platforms and you have to create a recognizable brand that reminds readers that they have enjoyed your work in the past and will likely enjoy it again.

Think of an actor who has a new movie coming out. In the months preceding its release in theaters, you will see the actor appearing on talk shows and making guest appearances on any number of programs to not just let the audience know that a new movie is about to be released, but to also remind the audience that the actor still exists. Promoting your written work on your blog is very similar to this, as you have to let readers know about new work by promoting it and you have to consistently remind readers that you exist by staying active and engaged in mediums beyond just your own site.

What Exactly Is Your "Brand"?

It is helpful to understand what exactly I mean when I use the term, "brand." I like to think of your brand as an amplified slice of your writing identity. This may seem a bit confusing, so allow me to explain: Your brand does not have to represent all of who you are, as it is indeed difficult -- and counterproductive -- to try to include every aspect of your unique personality in your brand. Instead, your brand should enable new readers to quickly understand what it is you are all about and should allow your preexisting readers to quickly and effortlessly recognize your new work.

Your brand is shaped by a number of factors, all of which are completely in your control. You are able to shape your brand identity through each of the following factors:

- "About the Author" section of your website
- Social media profiles
- Author bio for guest posts and freelance assignments
- Content of your articles and posts
- Contributions to comments section

Whenever you write an author bio or profile, remember that what you write will have a significant influence on the way readers -- and even editors -- perceive you and your work. Share who you are as a writer but be careful to include anything that might lead to misconceptions. You want your brand to be a positive reflection of who you are and what you believe in, so take some time to truly craft your brand so it is accurate and indicative of that part of yourself that identifies as a "writer."

Always Protect Your Brand and Your Reputation

While you are in almost complete control of your brand, the slightest misstep can be quite damaging. A piece of writing that comes off as insensitive or an offensive social media post (even if unintentional) can have serious consequences for your writing career. Even engaging in a silly argument in the comments section of your blog -- or even on some other website -- can have an effect on the way your readers perceive you, so take great care anytime you post anything.

One of the easiest ways to damage your reputation is by being uninformed. You have to protect your reputation and your brand and that means that you have to be sure that what you present as fact is verifiably accurate. Writers often engage in a race to publish first, but you are much better off confirming a fact before discussing it in a public forum. Always abide by professional standards, even when you are not necessarily functioning in a professional capacity.

Seek Out Opportunities to Contribute as a Guest Blogger

Now that we have discussed what branding is and some of the pitfalls involved in protecting your reputation, we can move on to the ways that you can build brand recognition by promoting your work. One of the most overlooked methods is through guest blogging opportunities. Most bloggers are more than happy to provide a forum for guest writers to publish their work as long as the subject matter is relevant to the site's content.

Some blogs will pay you for a guest post and others simply will not. This is completely irrelevant as a guest posting opportunity is beneficial solely in terms of the exposure it provides. New readers will see your work and most blogs will allow you to link back to your own site, and this type of promotion is invaluable. Of course, you have to make sure that you target sites that are likely to have readers who will be interested in your work.

Guest blogging also gives you an opportunity to build your resume and your portfolio through additional writing credits. You can show off your flexibility for future writing opportunities and demonstrate you are capable of intelligently discussing a broad range of subjects outside of your field of expertise. If you do guest blog, make sure that you offer the same opportunities on your site to other bloggers as well.

Take On Freelance Assignments for Established Publications

Freelancing for established publications offers many of the same benefits as guest blogging but provides a greater deal of legitimacy. These publications usually pay fairly well, but the standards are different and you will have to do a bit of research on each publication before you submit something or pitch an idea. Doing so will not only make it more likely that you are published, but it is also a necessary step in protecting your reputation.

There are many ways to research editorial guidelines for established publications, and the best resource is often the publication itself. Study the guidelines carefully and make sure that you strictly adhere to those guidelines, otherwise you may find it difficult to be taken seriously if you cannot follow explicit instructions. Make sure that your submission or pitch is representative of your best work and is clearly appropriate for the publication you have targeted.

Once you have been published in established publications, feel free to tactfully boast about it. You may want to simply update your author bio to include something like, "...whose work has been published in The New Yorker, The Atlantic and The Paris Review." How often your work appears in these publications is irrelevant, as once is enough to significantly boost your reputation. Just make sure you submit your work to varied publications and that you consistently maintain a sense of professionalism.

For example, it is not professional to fire off an angry e-mail to an editor telling them what a mistake they have made for passing on your work or how they will be embarrassed by their failure to recognize greatness. Instead, thank them kindly for taking the time to read your work and request constructive feedback while acknowledging that an editor of such a publication probably has very little time to do so. You probably will not get any feedback, but the editor will likely remember that you were polite, easy to work with and intent on refining your work. That will make it more likely that the editor will give your work a chance in the future or that you will receive at least some feedback if your work is again rejected.

A brief note on rejection: Get used to it! The New Yorker's rejection rate is something like 99.95 percent, and there are lots of reasons that your work may be rejected that have nothing to do with quality. Keep writing and submitting and do not worry about the opinions of others.

Be Active on Social Media

Create social media accounts across a variety of platforms and engage your readers on a regular basis. Maintain a sense of professionalism on social media at all times and only discuss topics relevant to the focus of your writing. We all have opinions on a variety of subjects, but it is best that you focus solely on your area of expertise when it comes to social media. Be creative, be engaging and be entertaining, but don't be controversial just to draw attention to yourself. Promote your work and have fun but do not do so at the expense of others.

Social media can be somewhat dangerous, and I have colleagues who avoid it altogether for this reason. It is a great promotional tool as long as you use it solely for professional reasons. Engage in intelligent discourse, let your readers know about the new work you have created and allow your readers to develop a sense of your personality through this type of communication. This will be exceptionally beneficial in building and promoting your brand in a positive manner.

Additional Considerations Concerning the Use of Social Media

In the previous chapter I touched on the importance of using social media. I believe that it is absolutely necessary for you to maintain a consistent presence on social media if you are to be successful as a professional blogger, but there are enough pitfalls in doing so that many of my peers in the writing community simply avoid it altogether. They may be able to get away with this because they are already established and have less of a need to self-promote, but social media is a tool that is essential for writers who are just beginning their career.

Understanding how to use social media properly is the key, so if you have used social media before or are currently active on one of the many platforms that currently exist you will have something of an advantage. For those who are new to social media, there is a bit of a learning curve, but it is not so steep that it is impossible to pick up quickly. Either way, I have some tips for using social media to benefit your professional writing career that should help you regardless of your previous social media experience.

When using social media to promote your work as a professional blogger, you have to do the following in order to be successful:

- Be active on a variety of social media platforms

- Be cautious regarding what you post
- Focus your activity on promoting your work
- Understand social media's unique language
- Be polite and professional at all times

Whether you enjoy social media or you despise it, the fact remains that it is an important tool for self-promotion that you will be better off for using. There will undoubtedly be some headaches that come with using social media, but the audience you are able to reach and engage is well worth any bit of difficulty you may encounter.

Frequently Use a Variety of Platforms

You are probably well aware that there are a variety of social media platforms out there, and it is simply not enough for you to be active on just one of them. While you may prefer Twitter to Facebook or Instagram, your readers have different preferences. You do not want to risk failing to reach someone because of your specific social media preferences, so be active on them all. Most writing platforms include a sharing tool that automatically alerts your followers when you have added a new post, but you also have to be engaging on social media to truly benefit.

This does not mean that you have to spend an hour each day posting to Facebook, Instagram, Twitter, Google+ or any other platform. Set up your site so that it sends out updates across all of your social media platforms and make an effort to be active on one of them each day. You will quickly figure out where most of your readers are and you can then devote more of your time to that specific social media platform. Just do not ignore the others, as you want to be as accessible as possible to your readers on all platforms.

Carefully Consider What You Post

This should really go without saying, but you have to be very cautious with regard to what you post on social media. Keep in mind that what you post is essentially permanent. How many times have you heard about someone posting something offensive or inflammatory only to delete it seconds later once the storm of criticism starts rolling in? For each one of those instances, how many times was the post saved and posted elsewhere? The second you post something there is someone there just waiting to save a screenshot, so be careful with regard to what you post online.

Remember, your social media presence is a major component of your brand and your identity. The best practice for maintaining a strong online reputation is to keep what you post relevant to your area of expertise while avoiding divisive and controversial subjects. If discussing divisive and controversial subjects is a major part of your writing, remember that there are limitations to these platforms that may make it difficult to thoughtfully explain your position. If you want to offer your insight on such a subject, simply link to an article that clearly lays out your position and your rationale, and do so politely.

Focus on Highlighting Your Work

It is vital that you remember why you are even using social media in the first place: to highlight the work that you have created. You may see many personal social media accounts engaging in general Internet silliness, but it is important for you to remember that your social media account is a professional account and not a personal account. You can have fun and be engaging while using social media, but remember that everything that you post should be somehow relevant to your work. That is why you have followers, after all. They want to know about you and your professional writing, but they may stop following you if you engage in some general Internet silliness or your posts are all over the place in terms of subject matter.

Grammatical and Structural Considerations

When using social media, you should understand that there is some shorthand involved and most casual users are not entirely concerned with the proper use of grammar at all times. As a writer, you should understand this shorthand but should also avoid using it with any frequency. If you feel the need to abbreviate something to squeeze it into Twitter's 140-character limit, for example, just post a link to your site instead of using shorthand. Using Internet shorthand may make you appear unprofessional, so avoid it at all costs.

Be Polite and Professional Above All Else

Social media is a great tool for writers to use in promoting their work and engaging their readers, and writers should always do this in the most professional and polite way possible. As a professional, you do not want to come across as crass or rude, and you certainly do not want to alienate any of your readers by treating them poorly online or dismissing what they have to say. In every online interaction consider the most polite response possible and go from there. This will ensure that you do not unintentionally hurt someone's feelings and that you are able to present yourself as a professional above all else.

Of course, you will very likely run into people who are simply trying to bait you into behaving in an unbecoming way just for sport. These people will direct offensive remarks your way and insult your work in the hope that you will profanely dismiss them or respond in kind by insulting them. Remember that someone who does this has no regard for their reputation and has nothing to lose by acting in this way. You, on the other hand, do have something to lose and do care about your reputation, so think twice before you respond to this sort of person. My advice is to thank them sincerely for their criticism and move on by electing to ignore them entirely. Engaging them further will only ensure that you inflict greater damage on yourself by making yourself seem unprofessional. Most platforms will allow you to block a specific user, so it is sometimes best to just offer your thanks and immediately block them before they are able to respond.

It should otherwise be your goal to engage in thoughtful discourse with your readers on subjects relevant to your writing. Always answer questions as honestly and directly as possible and allow your readers to feel as though they are an important part of your community. Accept suggestions and criticism from your audience with gratitude and try to show that you have used them in your writing somehow. My readers love that I introduce a topic they suggested by offering a brief word of thanks to the specific reader who made the suggestion. It doesn't take much effort on my part to acknowledge the suggestion, but it means an awful lot to the reader and it lets others know that I am willing to give credit where credit is due.

As a professional blogger, you will find that social media can be an excellent promotional tool that is also a wonderful way to communicate frequently with your audience. It is not without its drawbacks, of course, but by following the advice I have laid out you should be able to avoid any serious missteps in using social media. Always remember that everything you write plays a role in shaping your reputation as a writer, and this is true whether it is a 2,000-word article or a 140-character Twitter post. Simply be aware of this fact and make every effort to be polite and professional in order to reap all of the many rewards of using social media as a promotional tool.

Determining the Best Strategy for Monetizing Your Blog

You may be wondering why the chapter on monetizing your blog comes so late in this book, and there is good reason for the placement of this particular section. This is because the step that involves monetizing your blog is one that is fraught with the potential for error. It is my sincere belief that you should commit to building your blog and attracting an audience long before you ever consider monetizing your website. There are a variety of reasons for this, all of which I will explain in great detail in this chapter.

Once you are ready to begin profiting from your work you will have to make a decision with regard to how you will do so. There are countless options available to you, and some are much better than others. What works best for you and what is most appealing to your audience will vary according to the subject of your blog and the demographics of your audience, so I will merely explain these options and discuss the potential benefits and drawbacks of each:

- Leverage your expertise
- Affiliate marketing
- Direct advertising sales
- Banner advertising
- Paid product reviews

Some of these options may be less appealing to bloggers who are concerned with creating a conflict of interest.

Your integrity should always be of paramount importance and you should be cautious in applying a monetization strategy that creates this sort of conflict. Of course, it is possible to be completely forthright with your readers when it comes to some of these strategies, but you should still be careful to protect your integrity when in comes to generating revenue.

Considerations Before Moving to a Monetization Model

I completely understand why most bloggers are preoccupied with monetizing their website. After all, you are putting a lot of work into your website and you should certainly be compensated for doing so. My personal feeling is that there is a fair amount of risk involved in attempting to monetize too soon. If you load your website with advertising before developing your readership, the visitors to your site may question your legitimacy or they may have difficulty understanding how to navigate the site.

My suggestion is to build an audience first and then begin monetization efforts. You may have to wait some time before your site is profitable, but you will also make it more likely that you will generate greater revenue over the long-term and will be able to better leverage your position as an expert in your field if that is how you ultimately choose to monetize your website.

Leverage Your Position as an Expert

Once you have established an audience and demonstrated your impressive knowledge of your subject matter, you will be positioned well to profit from your reputation as an expert. There are a lot of ways to leverage your position as an expert, including:

- Products of your own creation (books, videos, podcasts, etc.)
- Speaking engagements
- Consulting services

Think of your blog as an online resume that includes detailed analysis of a variety of relevant subject matter. When you are able to consistently inform and entertain an audience through your blog, you will find that you are also able to charge for your expert analysis.

Whether that is through a speaking engagement or consulting services will depend upon the nature of the subject matter, but these opportunities exist in just about every field and subject area. Make sure that your website makes it clear that you offer these products and services and that there are clear instructions so any interested parties will know how to buy your products or otherwise benefit from your expertise.

Affiliate Marketing

There is a right way and a wrong way to approach affiliate marketing, and if you employ the right way it can be an excellent method for monetizing your website. Affiliate marketing is a relatively simple process in which you recommend a product to your audience and receive a cut of the profit any time one of your readers buys the product. You probably can see why this is a dicey process for monetizing your website, as there is a risk of creating a conflict of interest.

My advice is to use affiliate marketing infrequently and only when you would recommend the product to your readers anyway. The best way to ensure this is to simply write as you would normally write and if you happen to organically mention a product that you actually use, just check to see if the product has a program for affiliate marketing. If it does, use the program. If it doesn't, recommend the product anyway. This will help in protecting your integrity, but only to a degree.

The downside of affiliate marketing is that even when you actually believe in a product your readers will question whether or not you are just making the recommendation based on your potential for profit. You can add a disclaimer and completely disclose that you profit from your recommendation, but this will still raise questions about your integrity. Be very judicious when it comes to trading on your reputation in exchange for profit.

Direct Ad Sales or Banner Advertising

This type of advertising is probably the most commonly known strategy for monetizing a website, and there are two types of website advertising you can use:

- Direct ad sales
- Banner advertising

Direct ad sales will require a bit more effort on your part, but it is also the better option in terms of profit potential. Since you are selling the ad space directly to the advertisers you get to keep 100 percent of the sale, as opposed to the banner advertising programs that take a big cut -- often as large as 50 percent. Direct ad sales will also ensure that you remain in complete control of what appears on your blog since you will not be relying on an automated system like banner advertisers do.

Product Reviews

There are a lot of programs available that will pay you to review a product, but this is another risky way of monetizing your site. You can fully disclose that a specific post is a paid product review, but the fact that you are accepting money to review a product on your site may compromise your integrity despite your disclosure. Even when you believe a product is truly outstanding it will be hard for your readers to accept your opinion knowing that you have been paid to give it. Like affiliate marketing, you should be very careful in deciding whether or not to use this strategy as it could result in a loss of your core audience or cause harm to your reputation.

It is my opinion that you should exercise a great deal of patience when it comes to monetizing your site. It will undoubtedly be frustrating to put all that work into your site knowing that it is not yet generating revenue, but you have to take a long view and build a solid foundation that will ensure long-term profitability. After you have a sizable core readership in place and feel that you are ready to capitalize on all that hard work, be careful in choosing a method of monetization. After all, you have worked very hard to develop an excellent reputation as an expert in your field, so make sure you protect that reputation and generate revenue in a manner that is most suitable for continued success well into the future.

www.ingramcontent.com/pod-product-compliance
Lightning Source LLC
La Vergne TN
LVHW052316060326
832902LV00021B/3917